A DILLER,
A DOLLAR

Compiled by Lillian Morrison

YOURS TILL NIAGARA FALLS

BLACK WITHIN AND RED WITHOUT

A DILLER, A DOLLAR:
Rhymes and Sayings for the Ten O'Clock Scholar

TOUCH BLUE

REMEMBER ME WHEN THIS YOU SEE

SPRINTS AND DISTANCES:
Sports in Poetry and the Poetry in Sport

A DILLER
A DOLLAR

Rhymes and Sayings for the
Ten O'clock Scholar

Compiled by
Lillian Morrison

Illustrated by
Marj Bauernschmidt

Thomas Y. Crowell
Company • New York

Sixth Printing

For Bennette,
Gretchen,
and Lowell and Stephen

PREFACE

The main purpose of this collection of school verses and school children's lore is to amuse children, the young scholars who are now making such lore and passing it on. Arranged chiefly by subject of instruction, it takes somewhat the form of a mock primer.

There have been many changes in textbooks for the young since the days when American boys and girls learned the alphabet and The Lord's Prayer from a hornbook or pored over *The New England Primer*. But, although most textbooks are now large, colorful, and attractive, there has been little change over the years in the response of the child to "school." The reactions to the labor of learning, the constraint of the schoolroom, the agony of examinations, as expressed in rhyme or folk saying, have so far remained universal in spite of the strides (forward or backward, depending on one's opinion) of progressive education.

Except for a few of the longer pieces, almost all of the schoolroom plaints and schoolyard taunts, the mnemonics, proverbs and parodies, jokes and jingles, admonitions, game rhymes, and chants included here are true folklore. They are part of an ageless tradition and have come down to recent generations mainly by word of mouth. There is an almost primitive quality in many of the game rhymes and teasing rhymes which are passed on from child to child generation after generation—a strong suggestion of incantation in the sound of the words and a kind of remote ruthlessness in the meaning.

Some of the rhymes, we know for a certainty, are centuries old. The time-honored mnemonic, "Thirty days hath September" has been traced to Elizabethan times in English and to earlier versions in other languages. The ownership rhymes and grim warnings not to "steal this book" in the Book Inscriptions chapter are part of a tradition which goes back to the days, hundreds of years before the invention of printing, when the scribes in the early Christian monasteries added anathemas and other maledictions to manuscripts they had laboriously copied, as deterrents to anyone who might alter, destroy, or make away with the books. The rhymed lessons and proverbs in the Conduct of Life chapter recall the moralistic and didactic tone of so many books for children in the eighteenth and nineteenth centuries.

Although the rhymes vary in age and many give the flavor of early America, I have tried to choose those that have a freshness today and that reflect the irrepressible mischief, the love of pun and fun, the delightful sensitivity to sound, the inventiveness and vitality common to all childhood. Children and teen agers have given me orally a good many of the modern rhymes or modern versions of older ones. Adult friends and acquaintances who remembered rhymes from childhood have contributed. Autograph albums, still passed around by older boys and girls, have been an excellent source. Oldtime primers, chapbooks, collections of nursery rhymes, folklore journals, and other printed material have also served as sources. A list of those who contributed rhymes and information and a bibliography of printed sources will be found at the end of the book.

LILLIAN MORRISON

CONTENTS

ARITHMETIC

Two times one are two.
I know that as well as you.

Two times one is two;
Just keep still 'til I get through.
Three times three is nine;
You tend to your business and I'll tend to mine.

1, 2, 3, 4, 5, 6, 7,
All good children go to Heaven.
2, 3, 4, 5, 6, 7, 8,
All bad children have to wait.

Here comes teacher with a hickory stick;
You better get ready for arithmetic.

Forty sheep went through a gap,
Twenty white and twenty black.
Three times seven and twice eleven,
Three and two, how much is that?

(*Five*)

One, two,
Buckle my shoe;
Three, four,
Shut the door;
Five, six,
Pick up sticks;
Seven, eight,
Lay them straight;
Nine, ten,
A big, fat hen;
Eleven, twelve,
Dig and delve;
Thirteen, fourteen,

Maids a-courting;
Fifteen, sixteen,
Maids a-kissing;
Seventeen, eighteen,
Maids a-waiting;
Nineteen, twenty,
That's a-plenty;
Twenty-one, twenty-two,
That will do;
Twenty-three, twenty-four,
Say no more;
Twenty-nine, thirty,
Your face is dirty.

Twenty sick (six) sheep
Went up the gap;
One died,
How many came back?

(*Nineteen*)

1 for the money,
2 for the show,
3 to get ready, and
4 to go.

One's none,
Two's some,
Three's many,
Four's aplenty.

I love you a bushel,
I love you a peck,
I love you a hug
Around the neck.

I love you little, I love you lots;
My love for you would fill ten pots,
Fifteen buckets, sixteen cans,
Three teacups and four dishpans.

I'll sing you a song,
Nine verses long,
For a pin;

Three and three are six
And three are nine;
You are a fool,
And the pin is mine.

Make three-fourths of a cross,
Then a circle complete;
Let two semicircles
On a perpendicular meet.
Next add a triangle
That stands on two feet,
Then two semicircles
And a circle complete.

(TOBACCO)

8

When V and I together meet,
They make the number Six complete.
When I and V do meet once more,
Then these two letters make but Four.
And when that V from I is gone,
Alas, poor I can make but One.

To a semicircle, add a circle,
The same again repeat;
Add to these a triangle
And then you'll have a treat.

(COCOA)

The man in the wilderness said to me,
"How many strawberries grow in the sea?"
I answered him as I thought good,
"As many red herrings as grow in the wood."

Sixty seconds make a minute,
How much good can I do in it?
Sixty minutes make an hour,
All the good that's in my power.

When the weather's hot and burnin'
Tain't no time to be a learnin',
But when the ice is on the crick
That's the time for arithmetic.

Multiplication is vexation,
Division is as bad;
The Rule of Three, it puzzles me,
And fractions drive me mad.

If one and one are two,
And one and one do marry,
How is it in a year or two,
There's two and one to carry?

Thirty days hath September,
April, June, and November,
Save February; the rest have thirty-one
Unless you hear from Washington.

There were two birds sat on a stone,
One flew away and then there was one,
The other flew after and then there was none,
And so the poor stone was left all alone.

SPELLING

Come, dear teacher, hear me say
What I can of A B C.
A B C D E F G
H I J K LMNO P
Q R S and T U V
W and XYZ.
Now you've heard my A B C,
Tell me what you think of me.

A, B, C,
Double down D.
The cat's in the cupboard
And can't see me.

A—B, ab, catch a crab,
G—O, go, let it go.

While a baker was kneading his dough,
A weight fell down on his tough,
He suddenly exclaimed, "Ough!"
Because it had hurt him sough.

There was a hole in a hedge to get through;
It was made by no-one knew whough;
In getting through, a boy lost his shough,
And was quite at a loss what to dough.

Put i before e
Except after c,
Or when sounded like a,
As in neighbor and neigh;
And except seize and seizure
And also leisure,
Weird, height, and either,
Forfeit and neither.

A pretty deer is dear to me,
A hare with downy hair,
A hart I love with all my heart,
But barely bear a bear.

A little boy said, "Mother deer,
May eye go out two play?
The son is bright, the heir is clear;
Owe Mother, don't say neigh."

Bill had a billboard and also a board bill,
but the board bill bored Bill so that he
sold the billboard to pay the board bill.

An old lady living in Worcester
Had a gift of a handsome young rorcester,
But the way that it crough
As 'twould never get through,
Was more than a lady was uorcester.

An old couple living in Gloucester
Had a beautiful girl, but they loucester;
She fell from a yacht,
And never the spacht
Could be found where the cold waves had
    toucester.

My first is a circle,
My second a cross;
If you meet my whole,
Look out for a toss.

(o-x)

Do you realize that your real eyes tell real lies
    to me?

Constantinople is a mighty big word—
Can you spell it?
C-o-n con, I con if you con (can),
S-t-a-n stan, I stan if you stan (stand),
T-i ti, I ti if you ti (tie),
N-o no, I no if you no (know),
P-l-e ple, I ple if you ple (pull).

A cin and a natty,
A skinny and a fatty,
That's the way to spell Cincinnati.

Two O's, two N's, an L, and a D,
Put that together and spell it to me.

(*London*)

Spell Tennessee:
One-sy
Two-sy
Three-sy
Four-sy
Five-sy
Six-sy
Seven-sy
Eight-sy
Nine-sy
Ten-a-sy.

On a hill there is a mill,
From the mill, there is a walk,
Under the walk, there is a key.
Can you spell this name for me?

(*Milwaukee*)

Chicken in the car
And the car won't go.
That's the way to spell
Chicago.

P with a little o,
S with a t,
O double f,
And i-c-e.

(*Post Office*)

A knife and a fork,
A bottle and a cork.
That's the way to spell
New York.

Londonderry, Kirk, and Kerry,
Spell me that without a K.

(*T-h-a-t*)

Pease porridge hot,
Pease porridge cold,
Pease porridge in the pot,
Nine days old.
Spell me that without a P
And a clever scholar you will be.

(*T-h-a-t*)

What starts with a T,
Ends with a T,
And is full of T?

(*Teapot*)

England, Ireland, Scotland, Wales,
Monkeys, rats, and wiggle tails.
If you're the scholar I take you to be,
Put that together and spell it for me.

(I-t)

Thomas a Tattamus took two T's,
To tie two tups to two tall trees,
To frighten the terrible Thomas a Tattamus!
Tell me how many T's there are in all THAT.

(Two)

Apple pie, pudding, and pancake—
All begins with an A.

If I a lady think to be,
I first must learn my A, B, C.

He who ne'er learns his A, B, C,
Forever will a Blockhead be;
But he who to his Book's inclined
Will soon a golden Treasure find.

ENGLISH

(Grammar, Composition, and Punctuation)

Ain't ain't in the dictionary no more,
So I ain't gonna say ain't no more.
Ain't that good?

Oh, may I learn with true submission
Scott and Woolley's composition!

Heading for a letter:

> Jersey City,
> Jersey state,
> Excuse me, honey,
> I forgot the date.

As I was playing on the green,
A small English book I seen.
Carlyle's *Essay on Burns* was the edition
So I left it laying in the same position.

Sally Salter, she was a young teacher that taught,
And her friend, Charley Church, was a preacher
   who praught,
Though his friends all declared him a screecher
   who scraught.

27

The wind riz
And then it blew,
The rain friz
And then it snew.

Spring has sprung,
The grass has riz.
I wonder where
The flowers is?

Spring has sprung,
Fall has fell,
Winter's here
And it's cold as heck.

The swan swam over the sea,
Swim, swan, swim.
The swan swam back again;
Well swam, swan.

The sea ceaseth, but the forsythia sufficeth us.

The water fell down the mill dam, *slam*.
That's poetry.
The water fell down the mill dam, *helter-skelter*.
That's blank verse.

Of all the saws I ever saw saw, I never saw a saw
    saw like this saw saws.

A kiss is a noun
Both common and proper,
But not always approved
By mama and papa.

A kiss is a noun,
Standing up or sitting down,
Indicative mood, present tense,
Taken by those with common sense.

In the first person, simply *shall* foretells,
In *will* a threat or else a promise dwells;
Shall in the second and third does threat,
Will then simply foretells a future feat.

The following verses
make sense only when
punctuated correctly.

Example

King Charles the First
walked and talked.
An hour after,
was cut off.

King Charles the First walked and talked
Half an hour after his head was cut off.

I saw a peacock with a fiery tail
I saw a blazing comet drop down hail
I saw a cloud with ivy circled round
I saw a sturdy oak creep on the ground
I saw a pismire swallow up a whale
I saw a raging sea brim full of ale
I saw a Venice glass sixteen foot deep
I saw a well full of men's tears that weep
I saw their eyes all in a flame of fire
I saw a house as big as the moon and higher
I saw the sun even in the midst of night
I saw the man that saw this wondrous sight.

I saw a fishpond all on fire
I saw a house bow to a squire
I saw a parson twelve feet high
I saw a cottage near the sky
I saw a balloon made of lead
I saw a coffin drop down dead
I saw two sparrows run a race
I saw two horses making lace
I saw a girl just like a cat
I saw a kitten wear a hat
I saw a man who saw these too
And said though strange they all were true.

I saw a pack of cards gnawing a bone
I saw a dog seated on Britain's throne
I saw King George shut up within a box
I saw an orange driving a fat ox
I saw a butcher not a twelvemonth old
I saw a greatcoat all of solid gold
I saw two buttons telling of their dreams
I saw my friends who wished I'd quit these
     themes.

Every lady in this land
Has twenty nails upon each hand
Five and twenty on hands and feet
All this is true without deceit.

FOREIGN LANGUAGES

LATIN

Caesar adsum jam forte.

(Caesar had some jam for tea.)

Is ab ile, si ergo,
Fortibus es in ero.
Nobile themis trux,
Se vatacinum—causan dux!

(I say, Billy, see her go,
Forty buses in a row.
No, Billy, them is trucks,
See what's in 'em—cows and ducks!)

Darkibus nightibus no lightorum,
Boyibus kissibus sweet girlorum,
Popibus seeibus slapa girlorum,
Kickibus boyibus outa doororum,
Boyibus limpibus homa forlorum,
Girlibus cryibus kissa no morum.

Amo, amas,
I had a little lass;
Amas, amat,
She grew very fat;
Amat, amamus,
She grew very famous;
Amamus, amatis,
I fed her potatoes;
Amatis, amant
But she died of want.

Moods and tenses
Bother my senses;
Adverbs, pronouns, make me roar;
Irregular verbs
My sleep disturb,
They are a regular bore.

FRENCH

Je suis—I am a jar of jam,
Tu es—You are a fool,
Il est—He is the biggest jerk
That ever went to school.

Pas de lieu Rhône que nous.

(Paddle your own canoe.)

A GREEK BILL OF FARE

Legomoton,
Acapon,
Alfagheuse,
Pasti venison.

SLAVIC

Svidjanili afromsanit anisi
Yorlava Veniusi svidjanili,
Idchlitobodi siniginimar—iliol
Ogatinisatusi svidjanili.

(Sweet Jennie Lee from sunny Tennessee,
You'll love her when you see Sweet Jennie Lee,
Each little bird is singing merrily, all
Getting set to see Sweet Jennie Lee.)

Owata jollitimiv ad
Sinci tooklevov mioldad!

Oh what a jolly time I've had
Since I took leave of my old dad!

SPANISH

A E I O U

Mas sabe un burro que tu.

MORE TRANSLATIONS

Pound a feanut.
Fair 'dyou wind it?
Gin the utter.
Tot's it waste like?
Pike a leanut.

Maresy doats and dozy doats
And liddle lamzy divey;
A kiddley divey too,
Wouldn't you?

(Mares eat oats and does eat oats
And little lambs eat ivy;
A kid will eat ivy too,
Wouldn't you?)

In firtarris
In oaknunnis
In mudeelzar
In clainunnis.

(In fir tar is
In oak none is
In mud eels are
In clay none is.)

42

A B C D goldfish,
M N O goldfish.
O S A R D goldfish,
C M?
O I C.

(Abie, see the goldfish,
Them ain't no goldfish.
Oh, yes they are the goldfish,
See 'em?
Oh, I see.)

Captain B B B B
Sent his C C C C
To the D D D D
To dig O O O O O O O O.

(Captain Forbes
Sent his forces
To the fords
To dig potatoes.)

Stand	Take	2	Taking
I	U	Throw	My

(I understand you undertake to overthrow my
understaking.)

DRAWPU DNA DRAWNO

(*Read from right to left for translation*)

44

IXpect4U5

(I expect you between 4 and 5.)

If U B U and I B I
It's E Z 2 C the reason Y
I care 4 U,
B cause U R 2 Y's
2 T's me with your laughing I's.

CONCERNING THE
TEN COMMANDMENTS

P.RS.V.R.Y.P.RF.CTM.N
.V.RK..PTH.S.PR.C.PTST.N

(*To translate, substitute the letter e for the dots and
separate into words.*)

45

LOVE LETTER

He	One	Me	Same
Only	Only	Unto	The
Are	But	You	For
You	Love	Say	Me
And	I	And	Requite

She	One	He	One
Only	Only	Only	Only
Are	But	Am	But
You	Loves	I	Is
And	That	And	There

(Start from lower right and read up.)

SOCIAL STUDIES

The world is round, and like a ball
Seems swinging in the air,
A sky extends around it all,
And stars are shining there.

—Peter Parley

Is Russia Hungary?
I don't know. Alaska.

The Eskimo sleeps in his little bear skin
And sleeps very well, I suppose.
But once I slept in my little bare skin
And, by golly, I almost froze.

Geography, geography is such a pleasant study;
It tells us why the ocean's dry and why the
    desert's muddy.
I study it each morning, each afternoon, and then
I keep the teacher in so I can study it again.

If Mary goes far out to sea,
By wayward breezes fanned,
I'd like to know—can you tell me?
Just where would Maryland?

If Tenny went high up in air
And looked o'er land and lea,
Looked here and there and everywhere,
Pray what would Tennessee?

I looked out of the window and
Saw Orry on the lawn;
He's not there now, and who can tell
Just where has Oregon?

Two girls were quarreling one day
With garden tools, and so
I said, "My dears, let Mary rake
And just let Idaho."

A friend of mine lived in a flat
With half a dozen boys;

When he fell ill, I asked him why.
He said, "I'm Illinois."

An English lady had a steed.
She called him 'Ighland Bay.
She rode for exercise, and thus
Rhode Island every day.

Anonymous

Where did you get those pants?
Pantsylvania.
The coat?
North Dacoata.
The vest?
Vest Virginia.
The collar?
Collarado.
The hat?
Manhattan.
The shirt?
A fellow gave it to me.

What did Della wear?
She wore her New jersey.
Where has Orie gone?
He's taking Okla home.
What does Io weigh?
She weighs a Washing ton.
What does Ida hoe?
She hoes the Maryland.
How did Connecti cut?
She used the New Hamp shears.
What does Missis sip?
She sips her old Vir-gin.
How did Flori die?
She died of Mis-ery.
How did Wiscon sin?
He stole the New brass key.
What did Tenne see?
He saw what Arkan saw.
What did Massa chew?
He chewed his Old Kentuck.

In Fourteen Hundred and Ninety-two
Columbus sailed the ocean blue.
In Fourteen Hundred and Ninety-three
Columbus sailed the deep blue sea.
In Fourteen Hundred and Ninety-four
Columbus sailed the sea once more.

Columbus sailed from Palos, Spain,
Across the ocean blue,
Discovering San Salvador
In 1492.

Oh, the mighty king of France,
He marched his men to war,
But none of them got to the battlefield
Because it was so far.

The King of France
With twenty thousand men,
Went up the hill
And then came down again.
The King of Spain
With twenty thousand more
Climbed the same hill
The French had climbed before.

A-tisket, a-tasket,
Hitler's in his casket;
Eenie, meenie, Mussolini,
Six feet underground.

Shoot the cat,
Shoot the rat,
Shoot the dirty Democrat.

Shoot the turkey,
Shoot the hen,
Shoot the dirty Republican.

I often pause and wonder
At fate's peculiar ways;
For nearly all our famous men
Were born on holidays.

Queens and Kings
Are gaudy things.

NATURAL HISTORY

My dog Rover,
A clever little pup,
Stands on his hind legs
When you hold his front ones up.

The June bug has a gaudy wing,
The lightning bug a flame;
The bedbug has no wings at all
But he gets there just the same.

Way down yonder not so very far off,
A jaybird died with the whooping cough!
He whooped so hard with the whooping cough,
He whooped his head and his tail right off.

Did you ever go walking
On a warm summer day,
Walking by the water
Where the finny fishes play?
With their hands in their pockets
And their pockets in their pants,
Did you ever see the fishes
Do the hoochee-coochee dance?

I had a little pig,
I fed him in the trough.
He got so fat
His tail dropped off.

I've got a dog as thin as a rail,
He's got fleas all over his tail;
Every time his tail goes flop,
The fleas on the bottom all hop to the top.

Snail! snail! come out of your shell,
Or I'll beat on your back till you ring like a bell.
"I do very well," said the snail in the shell,
"I'll just take my chances in here where I dwell."

There's a grasshopper sitting on the railroad
    track,
Picking his teeth with a carpet tack.

On a mule you find two feet behind,
Two feet you find before;
You stand behind before you find
What the two behind be for.

Be kind to our web-footed friends,
'Cause a duck may be somebody's mother.
He lives all alone in the swamp, quack, quack,
Where it's cool and damp, quack, quack.
Now you may think that this is the end,
Well it is.

Roses are red,
Violets are blue;
The skunks had a college
And called it P. U.

Gooey, gooey was a worm,
A mighty worm was he;
He sat upon the railroad tracks,
The train he did not see.
Gooey, gooey!

Poor little fly on the wall
Walks upside down, he don't fall;
Ain't got no comb to comb his hair,
But fly don't care—
Ain't got no hair.

Inky, dinky spider
Climbed up the waterspout;
Down came the rain
And washed the spider out.
Up came the sun
And drove away the rain;
Inky, dinky spider climbed up the spout again.

Ladybug, ladybug, fly away home,
Your house is on fire, your children will burn;
All but the youngest, whose name is Ann,
And she hid herself 'neath the frying pan.

The cat doth play
And after slay.

The dog will bite
A thief at night.

The eagle's flight
Is out of sight.

Nightingales sing
In time of spring.

Cows give milk for food
That is very good.

The owl's delight
In time of night.

The ox calmly yields
To plow our fields.

The zebra wild
Is Afric's child.

64

HEALTH

An apple a day
Keeps the doctor away.
An onion a day
Keeps everyone away.

Early to bed,
Early to rise,
Makes a man
Healthy, wealthy, and wise.

Late to bed,
Early to rise,
Makes a man
Baggy under the eyes.

Early to bed,
Early to rise,
Gives you first choice
Of your old man's ties.

67

Full many a man, both young and old,
Is brought to his sarcophagus
By pouring water, icy cold,
Adown his warm esophagus.

After dinner rest a while,
After supper walk a mile.

Molly ate jam,
Molly ate jelly,
Molly went home
With a pain in her ———.
Now don't be mistaken,
Don't be misled,
Molly went home with a pain in her head.

Mary had a little lamb,
A little pork, a little jam,
A little fish, a little ham,
A little soda topped with fizz,
Now how sick our Mary is.

It's better to burp and bear the shame
Than spare the burp and bear the pain.

Sally drank marmalade,
Sally drank beer,
Sally drank everything
That made her feel queer.

A-whoopsie went the marmalade,
A-whoopsie went the beer,
A-whoopsie went everything
That made her feel queer.

A green little boy in a green little way
A little green apple devoured one day,
And the little green grasses now tenderly wave
O'er the little green apple boy's green little
    grave.

Down in Mississippi where I was born,
All I could eat was bread and corn;
I got so fat, I couldn't wear a hat,
So they hit me on the head with a baseball bat.

Tobacco is a nasty weed;
It's the devil that sows the seed;
Soils your pockets,
Scents your clothes,
And makes a chimney of your nose.

There was a young man from Morocco
Who smoked cigarettes by the stack-o,
And when he was dead,
They opened his head,
And found a big plug of tobacco.

How many bones in the human face?
Fourteen, when they're all in place.

There once was a lady who swallowed a fly.
I don't know why she swallowed the fly.
She'll probably die.

The same young lady swallowed a spider.
Imagine a spider crawling inside 'er.
She swallowed the spider to catch the fly.
Don't know why she swallowed the fly.
Of course she'll die.

Now this young lady swallowed a bird.
How very absurd to swallow a bird!
She swallowed the bird to catch the spider.
Imagine a spider crawling inside 'er.
She swallowed the spider to catch the fly.
Don't know why she swallowed the fly.
Of course she'll die.

Then the young lady swallowed a cat.
Imagine that—to swallow a cat!
She swallowed the cat to catch the bird.
How very absurd, to swallow a bird!
She swallowed the bird to catch the spider.
Imagine a spider crawling inside 'er.
She swallowed the spider to catch the fly.
Don't know why she swallowed the fly.
Of course she'll die.

The same young lady swallowed a dog.
She went whole hog when she swallowed the dog.
She swallowed the dog to catch the cat.
Imagine that—to swallow a cat!
She swallowed the cat to catch the bird.
How very absurd, to swallow a bird!
She swallowed the bird to catch the spider.
Imagine a spider crawling inside 'er.
She swallowed the spider to catch the fly.
Don't know why she swallowed the fly.
Of course she'll die.

Now this young lady swallowed a cow.
I don't know how but she swallowed a cow.

She swallowed the cow to catch the dog.
She went whole hog when she swallowed the dog.
She swallowed the dog to catch the cat.
Imagine that—to swallow a cat!
She swallowed the cat to catch the bird.
How very absurd, to swallow a bird!
She swallowed the bird to catch the spider.
Imagine a spider crawling inside 'er.
She swallowed the spider to catch the fly.
Don't know why she swallowed the fly.
Of course she'll die.

Then the young lady swallowed a horse.
She died, of course.

I sneezed a sneeze into the air;
It fell to the ground I know not where;
But hard and cold were the looks of those
In whose vicinity I had snoze.

Use three physicians still:
First, Dr. Quiet,
Next, Dr. Merryman,
And then, Dr. Diet.

SHORT STORIES

Mary Rose sat on a tack.
Mary Rose.

Owen More went away one day
Owen More than he could pay.
Owen More came back one day
Owen More.

I'll tell you a story
About Tom O'Nory
If you don't speak in the middle of it.
Will you?

"No."

The spell is broken,
You have spoken;
You'll never hear the story
Of long Tom O'Nory.

I went to the movies tomorrow
And took a front seat in the back;
I fell from the floor to the balcony
And broke a front bone in my back.

Mary, Mary,
Quite contrary,
Ate a cat
And ate a canary.
Now she goes to a special school
Because she is a special ghoul.

There once was a guy by the name of Jack,
Pitched his tent on a railroad track;
The 7:15 came round the bend.
What kind of flowers are you going to send?

Now, listen, my children and you shall hear
Of the midnight ride of Paul Revere.
He got in his car and stepped on the gas,
The bottom fell out and he fell on the grass.

So I said, "Old man, for whom digg'st thou this
    grave
In the heart of London Town?"
And the deep-toned voice of the digger replied,
"We're laying a gas-pipe down!"

I had a little calf
And that's half.
I put him in the stall
And tied him to the wall
And that's all.

Little Jack Horner sat in a corner
Watching the girls go by;
Along came a beauty. He said, "Hello, Cutie."
And that's how he got his black eye.

Solomon Grundy,
Born on a Monday,

Christened on Tuesday,
Married on Wednesday,

Took ill on Thursday,
Worse on Friday,

Died on Saturday,
Buried on Sunday.

This is the end
Of Solomon Grundy.

There were three ghostesses
Sitting on postesses
Eating buttered toastesses
And greasing their fistesses
Right up to their wristesses.
Weren't they beastesses
To make such feastesses?

He stood on the bridge at midnight
And tickled her face with his toes,
For he was only a mosquito
And he stood on the bridge of her nose.

They hurried down the lane, for it was late;
He ran before her to open the gate;
He tried to thank her, but didn't know how,
For he was a farmer and she was a cow.

Three children sliding on the ice,
Upon a summer's day,
As it fell out, they all fell in,
The rest they ran away.

Now had these children been at home
Or sliding on dry ground,
Ten thousand pounds to one penny
They had not all been drowned.

You parents all that children have
And you that have got none,
If you would keep them safe abroad
Pray keep them safe at home.

Once—but no matter when—
There lived—no matter where—
A man whose name—but then
I need not that declare.

He—well, he had been born,
And so he was alive;
His age—I details scorn—
Was somethingty and five.

He lived—how many years
I truly can't decide;
But this one fact appears,
He lived—until he died.

Moral

In this brief pedigree
A moral we should find;
But what it ought to be
Has quite escaped my mind.

Mary had a little lamb—
You've heard this tale before,
But have you heard she passed her plate
And had a little more?

There was an old soldier and he had a wooden
        leg;
He had no tobaccy, no tobaccy could he beg.
Another old soldier was as sly as a fox;
He always had tobaccy in the old tobaccy box.

Said the one old soldier, "Won't you give me a
        chew?"
Said the other old soldier, "I'll be danged if I do.
Save up your money and put away your rocks,
And you'll always have tobaccy in the old tobaccy
        box."

Well, the same old soldier was feelin' very bad.
He says, "I'll get even, I will, begad!"
He goes to a corner, takes a rifle from a peg,
And stabs the other soldier with a splinter from
        his leg.

I woke up one fine morning
And looked upon the wall.
The bedbugs and the cooties
Were having a game of ball.
The score was six to nothing,
The cooties were ahead,
The bedbugs made a home run
And knocked me out of bed.

Freddie filled his father's felt
With garlic, cheese, and boiled smelt;
When his father smelt the felt
He raised a welt on Freddie's pelt
With his Sunday meeting belt.

"Zaccheus he, did climb a tree,
His Lord to see."
The tree broke down and let him fall
And he did not see his Lord at all.

My story's ended,
My spoon is bended.
If you don't like it,
Go next door and get it mended.

CONDUCT OF LIFE

Before you say that ugly word,
Stop and count ten;
Then if you want to say that word,
Begin and count again.

A wise old owl lived in an oak;
The more he heard the less he spoke;
The less he spoke the more he heard.
Why can't we all be like that wise old bird?

Have communion with few,
Be familiar with one;
Deal justly with all,
Speak evil of none.

Ask me no questions,
And I'll tell you no lies;
But bring me those apples
And I'll make you some pies.

1, 2, 3, 4, 5, 6, 7,
All good children go to Heaven.
If you swear, you won't go there;
1, 2, 3, 4, 5, 6, 7.

It's not the looks,
It's not the shoes;
Pretty is
As pretty do's.

Dearly beloved brethren, is it not a sin,
When you peel potatoes to throw away the skin?
For the skin feeds pigs, and pigs feed you.
Dearly beloved brethren, is this not true?

You mustn't sing on Sunday
Because it is a sin,
But you may sing on Monday
Till Sunday comes agin.

Of a little, take a little;
Mind what you do.
Of a little, have a little;
So the rest can have some too.

Patience is a virtue,
Virtue is a grace,
And Grace is a little girl
Who doesn't wash her face.

Beautiful faces are they that wear
The light of a pleasant spirit there;
Beautiful hands are they that do
Deeds that are noble, good and true;
Beautiful feet are they that go
Swiftly to lighten another's woe.

Strive to keep the "Golden Rule"
And learn your lessons well at school.

He is a coward who will not turn back,
When first he discovers he's on the wrong track.

Still water runs deep,
Shallow water prattles;
The tongue hung in a hollow head
Rolls around and rattles.

A whistling girl and a crowing hen
Always come to some bad end.

Girls that whistle and hens that crow
Will always have fun wherever they go.

Learn to speak *slow;* all other graces
Will follow in their proper places.

Well begun
Is half done.

Let it not be said,
And said to your shame,
That all was beauty here
Until you came.

Keep this in mind, and all will go right
As on your way you go;
Be sure you know about all you tell
But don't tell all you know.

If you would have pleasure,
Your future adorning,
Be always good-natured
And up in the morning.

A man of words and not of deeds
Is like a garden full of weeds;
And when the weeds begin to grow
It's like a garden full of snow;
And when the snow begins to fall
It's like a bird upon the wall;
And when the bird begins to fly
It's like an eagle in the sky;
And when the sky begins to roar
It's like a lion at the door;
And when the door begins to crack
It's like a stick across your back;
And when your back begins to smart
It's like a penknife in your heart;
And when your heart begins to bleed
You're dead, and dead, and dead indeed.

In time take time while time doth last,
For time is no time when time is past.

Do as your mother bids you,
Do it with grace;
And if your fellow kisses you,
Slap him in the face.

In everything you do
Aim to excel,
For what's worth doing
Is worth doing well.

Stop! Look! and Listen!
Before you cross the street.
Use your eyes; use your ears;
Then use your feet.

For every evil under the sun
There is a remedy or there is none;
If there be one, try and find it,
If there be none, never mind it.

Don't look for the flaws as you go through life,
And even if you find them,
It is better and wise to be somewhat kind
And look for the virtues behind them.

To live with the saints in Heaven
Is untold bliss and glory,
But to live with the saints on earth
Is quite another story.

When you are old
And begin to scold,
Remember you never did
As you were told.

The path that once has been trod
Is never so rough to the feet,
And the lessons we once have learned
Are never so hard to repeat.

ETIQUETTE

Politeness is to do and say
The kindest thing in the kindest way.

I beg your pardon,
I grant your grace;
If you don't shut up,
I'll spit in your face.

Two's a couple,
Three's a crowd,
Four on the sidewalk
Is never allowed.

North is North,
South is South;
Keep your fingers
Out of your mouth.

The moon shines bright,
Can I see you home tonight?

The stars do too,
I don't care if you do.

If you must yawn, just turn aside
And with your hand the motion hide.
And when you blow your nose, be brief;
And neatly use your handkerchief.

Thy life to mend
This book attend.

BOOK INSCRIPTIONS

Inscriptions in history books

In case of fire, throw in.

If there should be another flood,
Then to this book I'd fly;
If all the earth should be submerged
This book would still be dry.

In Abraham Lincoln's arithmetic book

Abraham Lincoln,
His hand and pen,
He will be good but
God knows when.

In a notebook

Jack Thomas, 8th Grade, Section 6, Room 110,
Public School 12, Greenpoint, Brooklyn,
Kings County, New York, the United States,
America, the Northern Hemisphere, the World,
the Universe, Space, Private, Keep out,
this means YOU.

In a math book

Don't open till Christmas.

Who folds a leaf down,
The devil toast brown;
Who makes mark or blot,
The devil toast hot;
Who steals this book
The devil shall cook.

See these leaves aren't torn apart
Before this book is learned by heart.

Read slowly, pronounce carefully,
Pause frequently, think seriously,
Keep cleanly, return duly,
With the corners of the leaves not turned down.

The rose is red,
The grass is green,
And in this book
My name is seen.

If you steal this book, you risk your life,
For the owner carries a big jackknife.

If you keep this book you borrow,
May all your life be full of sorrow.

Whoever steals this book away
May think on that great Judgment Day
When the good Lord shall come and say,
"Where is that book you stole away?"
Then you will say, "I do not know."
And the Lord will say, "Go down below."

Black is the eye of the raven,
Black is the eye of the rook,
But blacker still will be the eye
Of him who steals this book.

This book is one thing,
My fist is another;
Touch this one thing,
You'll sure feel the other.

Don't steal this book, my honest friend,
For fear the gallows will be your end.
The gallows is high, the rope is strong,
To steal this book you know is wrong.

This book is one thing,
The gallows is another.
If you steal this thing
Depend upon the other.
Up the ladder, down the rope,
There you'll hang until you choke.

I pity the waiter,
I pity the cook,
I pity the one
Who steals this book.

Steal not this book, for if you do
Jim Higgins will be after you.

If I should chance to lose this book
And you should chance to find it,
Remember that my name is Bob—
MacDonald comes behind it.

If you dare to steal this book,
The devil will take you with his hook;
And if you say you do not care,
The devil will put you on a red-hot chair.

"Clap my hands and jump for joy;
I was here before Kilroy."

"Sorry to spoil your little joke;
I was here, but my pencil broke."
                              —Kilroy

If my name you want to see,
Turn to page 103.

On page 103: If my name you wish to discover,
Look eight pages from the cover.
If it is my name you lack,
Look six pages from the back.
If my name you want to know,
Look on page 1-4-0.

On page 140: If my name you cannot find,
Turn to page 79.

On page 79: Oh, you fool, you cannot find it,
Close the book and never mind it.

Bill Jones is my name,
U. S. is my nation,
Ohio is my dwelling place
And Heaven my expectation.

III

Sally Knox—her book;
God give her grace therein to look,
Not only look but understand
That learning is better than house or land.
When land is gone and money spent
Then learning is most excellent.

Let every lurking thief be taught,
This maxim always sure,
That learning is much better bought
Than stolen from the poor.
Then steal not this book.

If I this book do lend
And you it borrow,
Pray read it through today
And send it home tomorrow.

If this book should chance to roam,
Box its ears and send it home.

This book is not an orphan, so do not adopt it.

Whoever steals this book of knowledge
Will graduate from Sing Sing College.

He that takes this book of mine
Without my leave, commits a crime,
And to reward me for my trouble
Shall pay me four and twenty double.
The Scripture says but only four,
But I am poor and must have more.

My book and heart
Shall never part.

FAMOUS LAST WORDS

*(This section is dedicated
to the memory of those
who died waiting for the bell.)*

When I die, bury me deep,
Tell Taft High School not to weep,
Lay my math book at my head,
Tell Miss Barnes I'm glad I'm dead.

When I die, bury me deep,
Bury my history at my feet,
Tell my teacher I've gone to rest,
And won't be back for the history test.

I never went to Harvard,
I never went to Yale,
I got my education
At the Hudson County Jail.

Fail now and avoid the June rush.

Let all who would these pages scan,
Learn the fate of this poor man:

Here lies
the miserable body
of poor
Henry Brown Esq.

who was placed
in the Baxter School
by a Cruel Parent
and allowed
to DIE
from too much
FRENCH

If at first you don't succeed, slide for second.

Many are cold, but few are frozen.

I went to Rosie's funeral,
I heard the preacher say,
"Here lies the shell,
The nut has passed away."

Roses are red,
Violets are blue,
I copied your paper,
And I flunked too.

When I am dead and in my grave
Remember the girl who didn't behave.

When you come past my grave
And I am dead and rotten,
Just hold your nose
And keep on trottin'.

Did you ever think when the hearse goes by
That you may be the next to die;
That you'll be riding in a big black hack
And you won't be thinking of coming back.
They'll wrap you up in a big white sheet
And bury you down about six feet.
All goes well for about one week
And then the coffin begins to leak.
The worms crawl in and the worms crawl out
They play pinochle on your snout.
You never thought that when you die
The worms would eat you like eating pie.

Don't bother me now,
Don't bother me never,
I want to be dead
For ever and ever.

Our days begin with trouble here,
Our life is but a span,
And cruel death is always near,
So frail a thing is man.

Poor ink,
Poor pen,
Poor me,
Amen.

TEACHER, TEACHER

I'm a little curly head,
My father is a preacher.
I love to go to Sunday School
And listen to my teacher.

Had a little wooden gun,
Shot a rabbit on the run,
Skinned him on the Sabbath day.
Oh what will my teacher say?

'Kingsbridge is my station,
United States is my nation.
I go to school to act the fool
And that's my education.

Hickory leaves and calico trees,
All schoolteachers are hard to please.

You can lead a horse to water,
But you cannot make him drink.
You can send a fool to college,
But you cannot make him think.

Little bits of nerve,
Little grains of sand,
Make the biggest blockhead
Pass a hard exam.

Dr. Faustus was a very good man,
He whipped his scholars now and then.
When he whipped them, he made them dance
Out of Scotland into France,
Out of France into Spain,
And then he whipped them back again.

Doctor Long is a very good man,
He tries to teach you all he can,
Reading, writing, and 'rith-ma-tick,
But he never forgets to use the stick.

All the curse words on the earth,
All those that I've learned from birth
Couldn't express what I feel for you,
Liking Miss Hayward the way you do.

Roses are red,
Violets are blue,
You like Miss Jackson,
So phooey to you.

Teacher, teacher made a mistake,
She sat down on a chocolate cake!
The cake was soft,
Teacher fell off.
Teacher, teacher made a mistake.

Do, re, me, fa—mi
My teacher's balmy.
He's gone to join the army,
Do, re, mi, fa—mi.

The more we study, the more we know.
The more we know, the more we forget
The more we forget, the less we know.
The less we know, the less we forget.
The less we forget, the more we know.
Why study?

Here I stand
All ragged and dirty.
If teacher should kiss me,
I'd run like a turkey.

Remember A,
Remember B,
Remember the Education Fee,
Ten dollars.

Tattle tale, teacher's pet!
Tell it quick or you'll forget.

Monkey see, monkey do,
Copy cat number two.

A dillar, a dollar,
A ten o'clock scholar,
What makes you come so soon?
You used to come at ten o'clock,
And now you come at noon.

Ashes to ashes,
Dust to dust,
Oil those brains
Before they rust.

Roses are red,
Violets are blue,
And this is the zero
I give to you.

April Fool,
Go to school,
Tell your teacher,
She's a fool.

Teacher, Teacher,
I declare,
I see Mary's underwear.

Hot roasted peanuts
Tell the teacher she's nuts.
If she asks you what's your name
Tell the teacher she's a pain.

8 years of grammar,
4 years of high,
2 years of college,
And you're ready to die.

If dumbness were an occupation,
You would be a great sensation.

Now you are graduating,
Isn't that fine!
You've been in the eighth grade
Since 1909.

He who in Learning takes Pride
In Coach and Six may chance to ride,
While every Dunce's life must be
A scene of servile Drudgery.

IN THE SCHOOLYARD

I made you look,
I made you look,
I made you buy a penny book.

I made you sigh,
I made you sigh,
And pretty soon I'll make you cry.

Red and yellow,
Catch a fellow.
Blue and white,
Squeeze him tight.

Cheating shows,
Never goes.
The devil's right behind you.

I'll tell Mom when I get home,
The boys won't let the girls alone;
They pull their hair, they break their bones,
I'll tell Mom when I get home.

Rain, come wet me;
Sun, come dry me;
Go 'way, Susie,
Don't come nigh me.

Smarty, smarty, smarty,
Thought you'd have a party.
Don't forget what the teacher taught,
You'll be sorry if you get caught.
I'm going to tell your mother,
Now see if you don't care,
You're nothing but a smarty cat
So there, there, there.

Red, white, and blue,
I don't speak to you.

Take off your left shoe,
And I can tell your fortune:
I'll tell you what your trouble is;
I'll tell you who wants you;
I'll tell you who loves you.

God loves you,
The devil wants you,
And the trouble is to put on your shoe.

Sticks and stones may break my bones,
But names will never hurt me.
When I die, then you'll cry
For the names you called me.

Cry, baby, cry,
Stick your finger in your eye,
Tell your mother it wasn't I.

I asked my mother for fifty cents
To see the elephant jump the fence.
He jumped so high, he touched the sky
And didn't get back till the Fourth of July.
The Fourth of July, a punch in the eye,
And that's what you get for telling a lie.

Pins and needles,
Needles and pins,
Sass me again
And I'll kick your shins.

Liar, liar, lick spit,
Your tongue shall be slit,
And all the dogs in town
Shall have a little bit.

Liar, liar,
Your pants are on fire;
Your nose is as long
As a telephone wire.

Flypaper, flypaper,
Gooey, gooey, gooey,
Flypaper, flypaper,
Hope it sticks on Louie.

A rolling stone gathers no moss;
What care I for the friend I lost.
Pass her by, let her see
There's far more chums in the world for me.

Birds of a feather flock together
And so will pigs and swine;
Rats and mice will have their choice,
And so will I have mine.

Billy, Billy is no good,
Chop him up for fire wood;
If the fire does not burn
Billy is a big fat worm.

Cross my heart and hope to die,
Eat a banana and holler Hi!

Fat, fat, the water rat,
Fifty bullets in his hat.

Fatty, fatty,
Two by four,
Swinging on the kitchen door.
When the door began to shake
Fatty had a bellyache.

Johnny's it,
And got a fit,
And couldn't get over it.

What's your name?
Pudding and Tame,
Ask me again and I'll tell you the same.
Where do you live?
Down the lane.
What's your number?
Cucumber.

What's your name?
Buster Brown.
Ask me again
And I'll knock you down.

My name's West,
I ain't in this mess.

"Where do you live?"

"On Tough Street. The farther you go, the tougher they get; I live in the last house."

"What time is it?"

"Time all fools were dead. Ain't you sick?"

When someone says, "Hey!":

> Hay is for horses,
> Straw is for cows,
> Milk is for babies
> For crying out loud.

or

> Hey!
> Straw.
> What you can't eat,
> You may gnaw.

"Curiosity killed a cat."
"Satisfaction brought it back."

143

"May I see that?"
"No sea on it, all dry land."

When someone objects to your staring, you say:

A cat may look at a king,
And surely I may look at an ugly thing.

SCHOOL'S OUT

When cold and dismal is the dawn
And days are dark and drear,
I like to think of all the roads
That lead away from here.

Tonight, tonight,
The pillow fight,
Tomorrow's the end of school.
Break the dishes, break the chairs,
Trip the teachers on the stairs.

No more pencils, no more books
No more teachers' nasty looks.

No more Latin, no more French,
No more sitting on a hard school bench.

No more homework, oh what cheer
No more school for the rest of the year!

147

ACKNOWLEDGMENTS

I am especially grateful to Mrs. Elizabeth Pilant and the National Conference American Folklore for Youth at Ball State Teachers College, Muncie, Indiana, for twenty-seven selections from their mimeographed collection of American autograph rhymes. Many thanks also to the following children, adult friends, colleagues in The New York Public Library, and other kind contributors, for rhymes or information leading to the rhymes included in this book: Eleonora Botti, Maureen Boult, Mrs. Barbara Perkins Brownlow, Mrs. Margaret Taylor Burroughs, Theresa K. Casile, Frieda and Ruth Coren, Kevin Duffy, Monica Foley, John Gonzalez, Esther Gorey, Linda Grant, Morris Hadley, Ida Heinzmann, Janet Hermann, Gilbert Highet, Mollie Horton, Mrs. Philomena Casella Houlihan, Joan Howard, Nancy Huyett, Khadijah Ismail, Bruce Jackson, Mrs. Margaret Lamont Landes, Mrs. Edna Levine, Katherine Love, Gerald McDonald, Mrs. Maxine McKay, Constance Marzullo, Helen Masten, Mrs. Gene Megerian, Mrs. Margaret D. Mellars, Gertrude Moakley, Amelia Munson, Jerry Nedwick, A. Margaret Nellis, Mildred Nelson, Sara Jane Ornstein, Mrs. Esther Walls Pappy, Mrs. Josephine Perkins, Margaret Rodd, Mr. and Mrs. Alvin A. Samuels, Mrs. Sylvia Schwartz, Margaret Scoggin, Sylvia Sims, Catherine Stiscia, Lena Otie Toms, Alexandra Weinstein, Mrs. Frances Carnes Weintraub, Mrs. Pura Belpré White, Carl Withers, Andrew Wright, and a few children whose names I never knew.

BIBLIOGRAPHY

Before naming printed sources, I wish to express my indebtedness to and appreciation for the great resources of The New York Public Library whose Main Reading Room, American History Division, Rare Book Room, Teachers' Library Branch, and Central Children's Room have supplied almost all the material listed below.

Allison, Leah. "Traditional Verse from Autograph Books," *Hoosier Folklore*, vol. 8, no. 4, 1949.

The Alphabet. New York: Mahlon Day, 1840(?).

Averill, Laurence A. *Adolescence: a Study in the Teen Years*. Boston: Houghton Mifflin, 1936.

Barber, Marshall A. *The Schoolhouse at Prairie View*. Lawrence, Kansas: University Press, 1953.

Bergen, Fanny D. "Flyleaf Rhymes and Decorations," *New England Magazine*, vol. 23, no. 5, 1901.

Brewster, Paul G. "The Friendship Verse, a Hardy Perennial," *Hoosier Folklore*, vol. 5, no. 3, 1946.

———. "Smart Sayings," *Hoosier Folklore*, vol. 6, no. 2, 1947.

Brower, Lesley. "Two Jingles," *New York Folklore Quarterly*, vol. 1, no. 2, 1945.

Bryant, Margaret M. "Folklore in the Schools; Folklore in College English Classes," *New York Folklore Quarterly*, vol. 2, no. 4, 1946.

Crampton, Gertrude. *Your Own Joke Book*. New York: Comet Books, 1948.

English as She Is Wrote. New York: Appleton, 1884.

Forbes, Edith Emerson. *Favourites of a Nursery of Seventy Years Ago*. Boston: Houghton Mifflin, 1916.

Gammer Gurton's Garland: or the Nursery Parnassus. London: R. Triphook, 1810.

Green, Edward. "Riddles from South Antrim," *Bealoideas*, vol. 11, no. 1, 1941.

Greenleaf, Elizabeth B. "Riddles of Newfoundland," *The Marshall Review*, vol. 1, no. 3, 1938.

Halliwell-Phillipps, J. O. *The Nursery Rhymes of England*. London: Frederick Warne, 1886.

———. *Popular Rhymes and Nursery Tales*. London: John Russell Smith, 1849.

Halsey, Rosalie V. *Forgotten Books of the American Nursery*. Boston: Goodspeed, 1911.

Hyatt, Harry Middleton. *Folklore from Adams County, Illinois*. Memoirs of the Anna Egan Hyatt Foundation. New York: 1935.

Johnson, Clifton. *Old-time Schools and School-books*. New York: Macmillan, 1917.

Kennedy, Charles O'Brien. *A Treasury of American Ballads*. New York: McBride, 1954.

Loomis, C. Grant. "Traditional American Wordplay," *Western Folklore*, vol. 8, no. 4, 1949.

Marmaduke Multiply's Merry Method of Making Minor Mathematicians. London: J. Harris, 1817.

McCord, David. *What Cheer*. New York: Coward-McCann, 1945.

Millard, Eugenia L. "Sticks and Stones," *New York Folklore Quarterly*, vol. 1, no. 1, 1945.

Newell, William Wells. *Games and Songs of American Children*. New York: Harper, 1884.

The New England Primer. Boston: E. Draper, 178-(?).

Opie, Iona and Peter. *I Saw Esau*. London: Williams and Norgate, 1947.

————. *The Oxford Dictionary of Nursery Rhymes*. Oxford: Oxford, 1952.

The Picture Riddler. Boston: G. W. Cottrell, 1845.

Potter, Charles Francis. "Autograph Album Rimes," *Funk & Wagnalls Standard Dictionary of Folklore, Mythology and Legend*, vol. 1, 1949.

Quinn, Hugh. "Folklore in the News," *Western Folklore*, vol. 10, no. 1, 1951.

Repplier, Agnes. *In Our Convent Days*. Boston: Houghton Mifflin, 1933.

The Royal Alphabet, or Child's Best Instructor. Boston: Samuel Hall, 1795(?). Repr. Philadelphia: Lippincott, 1942.

Smith, Grace Partridge. "Folklore from 'Egypt,'" *Hoosier Folklore*, vol. 5, no. 2, 1946.

Talley, Thomas W. *Negro Folk Rhymes, Wise and Otherwise*. New York: Macmillan, 1922.

Taylor, Archer. *The Proverb*. Cambridge: Harvard University Press, 1931.

Thompson, Lawrence S. "A Cursory Survey of Maledictions," *Bulletin of The New York Public Library*, vol. 56, no. 2, 1952.

Walsh, William Shepard. *Handy-book of Literary Curiosities*. Philadelphia: Lippincott, 1925.

Waugh, F. W. "Canadian Folklore from Ontario," *Journal of American Folklore*, vol. 31, no. 119, 1918.

Wells, Carolyn. *Such Nonsense*. New York: George Doran, 1918.

Wilson, Marguerite Ivins. "Yours Till—," *Utah Humanities Review*, vol. 1, no. 3, 1947.

Wood, Ray. *Fun in American Folk Rhymes*. Philadelphia: Lippincott, 1952.